Animals of North America
CARIBOU

by Tammy Gagne

FOCUS
READERS

North Star
EDITIONS

www.northstareditions.com

Produced for North Star Editions by Red Line Editorial.

Photographs ©: Jeff McGraw/Shutterstock Images, cover, 1, 4–5, 27 (bottom left); Red Line Editorial, 6; Sergey_Krasnoshchokov/Thinkstock, 8–9; Ron Sanford/iStockphoto, 11; Iakov Filimonov/Shutterstock Images, 12, 29; Gooddenka/iStockphoto, 14–15; Design Pics/Thinkstock, 17; Zamytskiy Leonid/Shutterstock Images, 19; kjekol/iStockphoto, 20–21; Troutnut/Shutterstock Images, 22–23; Jeff McGraw/iStockphoto, 24; mkubista/Thinkstock, 27 (top); akphotoc/Shutterstock Images, 27 (bottom right)

ISBN
978-1-63517-033-7 (hardcover)
978-1-63517-089-4 (paperback)
978-1-63517-192-1 (ebook pdf)
978-1-63517-142-6 (hosted ebook)

Library of Congress Control Number: 2016951008

Printed in the United States of America
Mankato, MN
November, 2016

About the Author

Tammy Gagne has written more than 150 books for adults and children. She resides in northern New England with her husband and son. One of her favorite pastimes is visiting schools to talk to kids about the writing process.

TABLE OF CONTENTS

CHAPTER 1

LONG-DISTANCE TRAVELERS

Caribou can survive in extremely cold weather. They spend much of their time in **tundra** regions of North America. They also live in swampy forests called **taiga**.

Caribou are a kind of large deer.

Pacific Ocean · Arctic Ocean · Europe · North America · Atlantic Ocean · Asia · Pacific Ocean · Indian Ocean

N W E S

 where caribou live

Caribou also live in northern areas of Europe and Asia.

In winter, caribou **migrate**. They go as far as southern Canada and the northern United States. They travel back north in summer.

Caribou live in large groups called **herds**. A female caribou is a doe.

A male is a buck. When migration begins, does leave first. The bucks make their journey several weeks later with the older **calves**. They follow the same paths. These routes are worn down from the animals' yearly trips.

FUN FACT

A caribou can travel as far as 1,600 miles (2,574 km) in one year.

CHAPTER 2

ANTLERS AND HOOVES

Caribou are mostly brown. They have white fur on their necks, bellies, and rumps. Their stocky bodies are covered in thick fur. Their coats keep them warm during cold winters.

A buck's antlers are bigger than a doe's.

Caribou stand from 4 to 5 feet (1.2 to 1.5 m) tall at their shoulders. Their long legs help them move through deep snow.

Caribou have strong hooves. These hooves help support a caribou's heavy body on snow or swampy land.

FUN FACT

The bottoms of a caribou's hooves are hollow. Caribou use their hooves as shovels to dig through snow.

 **Most caribou weigh between 240 and 700 pounds (109 and 318 kg).**

PARTS OF A CARIBOU

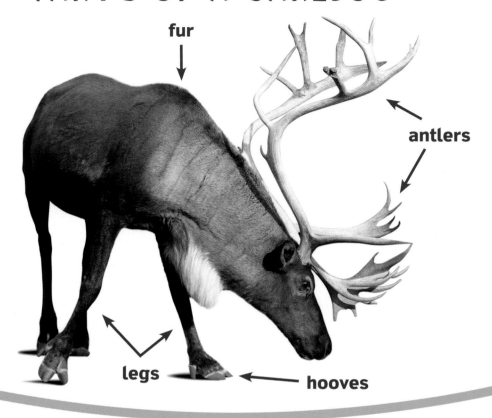

fur

antlers

legs

hooves

Hooves also help caribou swim across waterways. Caribou use their hooves to paddle in water.

Both bucks and does have antlers. Caribou are the only deer species in which this happens. Bucks and does use their antlers to defend their territory. Does also use them to fight off **predators** that threaten their young.

FUN FACT

Bucks shed their antlers each winter. They grow new ones every spring.

CHAPTER 3

BUILT TO SURVIVE

Caribou have many traits that help them survive. Predators such as bears and wolves hunt caribou. A herd has a much better chance of avoiding an attack than a single animal does.

 Living in a herd helps caribou stay alive.

A caribou's coat helps it survive in a different way. The hairs are hollow, much like tiny straws. These hairs trap air, which keeps the caribou warm. The air also helps the caribou float. This helps the caribou swim.

A caribou's coat and hooves help it swim.

Caribou have a trait that helps them survive when food is scarce. Most animals cannot eat **lichen** without getting sick. But caribou have certain **bacteria** in their guts. These bacteria allow the caribou to digest lichen safely.

FUN FACT

A hungry caribou can smell lichen under as much as 5 feet (1.5 m) of snow.

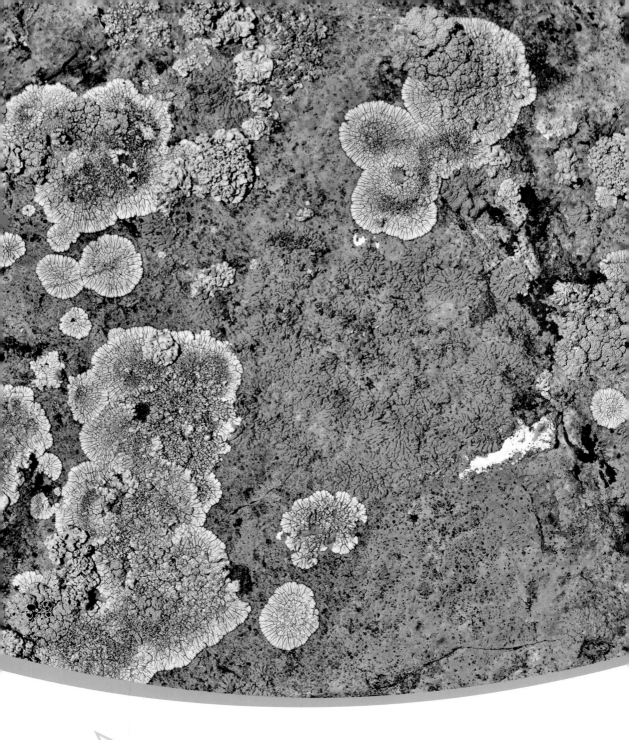

The tundra is filled with lichen.

HOLDING ON TO HEAT

We often see the air people exhale through their noses in cold weather. This happens because the air leaving the human body is so warm. But we can't see the air a caribou breathes out of its nose. It isn't visible even when the temperature dips to −22 degrees Fahrenheit (−30°C). This is because the animal holds on to the heat from the air it breathes in before exhaling. This keeps the caribou warm.

Caribou are able to adapt to freezing temperatures.

CHAPTER 4

LIFE IN THE HERD

Caribou are nomadic animals. They spend their entire lives moving from one place to another. They move wherever they can to find food.

Caribou decide where to go based mostly on food.

 **Caribou are herbivores, eating only plants and lichen.**

Caribou use a lot of energy traveling so far each season. When they reach the tundra each spring, caribou begin eating as much as possible. Lichen is not high in **nutrients**. Grasses and plants offer more nutrients. Caribou also eat fruits and twigs.

Around October, bucks begin to compete. They fight for the attention of does. Calves are born approximately eight months later.

FUN FACT

An adult caribou can eat 12 pounds (5.4 kg) of food each day.

A mother caribou usually has one or two calves at a time. Each one weighs approximately 10 pounds (4.5 kg) at birth. It can stand 30 minutes after it is born. Calves stay with their mothers through the summer. They are ready to live on their own by the fall. Wild caribou usually live 15 years.

FUN FACT

Caribou can run up to 50 miles per hour (80 km/h).

CARIBOU LIFE CYCLE

One or two calves are born to a mother caribou.

Calves spend the summer with their mothers.

Even though they are part of a herd, adult caribou can live independently.

FOCUS ON
CARIBOU

Write your answers on a separate piece of paper.

1. Write a sentence that describes the key ideas from Chapter 2.

2. If you could have one, do you think a caribou would make a good pet? Why or why not?

3. Where is one place caribou have white fur?

    A. hooves

    B. antlers

    C. rumps

4. Why do you think caribou eat as much as possible when they reach the tundra each spring?

    A. They want to eat up all of the food sources in the area.

    B. The migration took a lot of energy, and the caribou need food for energy.

    C. They don't know when they might get to eat again.

5. What does **nomadic** mean in this book?

    A. roaming

    B. stationary

    C. lazy

Caribou are **nomadic** animals. They spend their entire lives moving from one place to another.

6. What does **hollow** mean in this book?

    A. filled

    B. empty

    C. flexible

The hairs are **hollow**, much like tiny straws. These hairs trap air, which keeps the caribou warm.

Answer key on page 32.

GLOSSARY

bacteria
Microscopic, single-celled living things that can either be useful or harmful.

calves
Young caribou.

herds
Groups of animals that stay together.

lichen
A plant-like material made of algae and fungus.

migrate
To move from one region to another at the change of the seasons.

nutrients
Substances humans, animals, and plants need to stay strong and healthy.

predators
Animals that hunt other animals for food.

taiga
A damp region filled with cone-producing trees.

tundra
A treeless plain in the arctic filled with mosses and small shrubs.

TO LEARN MORE

BOOKS

Hirsch, Rebecca E. *Caribou: A Tundra Journey*. New York: AV2 by Weigl, 2017.

Jeffries, Joyce. *Caribou*. New York: PowerKids Press, 2016.

Markovics, Joyce L. *Caribou and Reindeer, Too*. New York: Bearport Publishing, 2011.

NOTE TO EDUCATORS

Visit **www.focusreaders.com** to find lesson plans, activities, links, and other resources related to this title.

INDEX

A
antlers, 13

B
bucks, 7, 13, 25

C
calves, 7, 25–27

D
does, 6–7, 13, 25

F
fur, 9

H
herd, 6, 15, 16, 27
hooves, 10, 12

L
legs, 10, 16
lichen, 18, 25

M
migrate, 6–7

P
predators, 13, 15, 16

T
taiga, 5
tundra, 5, 24